I0490644

From Idea to Reality:

The Complete Start-Up Handbook

CLAUDIA LOWRY

From Idea to Reality: The Complete Start-Up Handbook

Copyright © 2023 Every Task LLC
All rights reserved.
ISBN: 9798386868420

TABLE OF CONTENTS

Introduction

Starting a business can feel overwhelming, especially for those new to entrepreneurship. Turning an idea into a tangible, profitable business requires a thorough understanding of the market, legal and financial requirements, and the ability to execute a business plan effectively. "From Idea to Reality" serves as an all-encompassing guide for entrepreneurs at every stage of the start-up process.

With practical advice and step-by-step instructions, "From Idea to Reality" offers an overview of essential topics such as conducting market research, identifying funding sources, developing a solid business plan, and branding a new company. The book also covers intellectual property protection, legal and tax considerations, and hiring employees.

While launching a start-up can be challenging, "From Idea to Reality" helps entrepreneurs navigate each step confidently. By providing a comprehensive understanding of the start-up process and offering practical solutions for everyday challenges, this book empowers entrepreneurs to turn their ideas into successful businesses.

Overall, "From Idea to Reality" is an essential resource for anyone looking to start a business. It offers practical insights and actionable steps to help aspiring entrepreneurs achieve their goals and build their dreams into reality.

Chapter One
Introduction: How to Turn Your Idea into a Successful Startup

Turning your idea into a successful startup is a challenging task. Many entrepreneurs have great business ideas, but they need help executing them. While starting a business requires effort, dedication, and risk-taking, it also requires a well-designed strategy and a clear market understanding.

Entrepreneurship is not just about making money; it's about creating value. Before starting a business, you must ask yourself if your idea will solve a problem or meet a need. Your startup should aim to make people's lives better or easier. You need to evaluate if your idea has the potential to scale.

The first step in turning your idea into a successful startup is conducting market research. You must understand the market, identify your target audience, and analyze your competition. You can use different tools and methods to gather information, such as surveys, interviews, and focus groups. This will help you to determine if there is a demand for your product, what features are essential, and how much customers are willing to pay.

Once you have validated your idea, the next step is to create a business plan. A business plan is a roadmap that outlines your goals, strategies, and financial projections. It should include your mission statement, product description, market analysis, marketing plan, financial plan, and funding requirements. Your business plan will help you to stay focused on your goals, convince investors to fund your startup, and evaluate your progress.

After creating a business plan, you need to register your business. This includes recording your business name and structure, obtaining licenses and permits, and registering for taxes. It is essential to have a legal system that protects you from personal liability in case of any legal issues.

The next step is to build your team. You need to hire people who share your vision and have the required skills to execute your business plan. You can hire employees or work with freelancers depending on your budget and business needs.

Once you have your team, you must develop your product or service. This includes designing, manufacturing, or creating your product, testing it, and refining it based on customer feedback. You must also develop a marketing strategy to promote your product and build brand awareness.

Finally, it would be best if you launched your startup. This includes developing a launch plan, setting up your website and social media accounts, and reaching potential customers. Again, it would be best to have a solid launch plan to impact the market and attract customers significantly.

In conclusion, turning your idea into a successful startup requires hard work, dedication, and a clear market understanding. You must conduct market research, develop a business plan, register your business, build your team, develop your product, and launch your startup. With the right strategy and execution, you can turn your business idea into a successful startup.

Chapter Two
Building a Successful Business Plan from Scratch

Starting a new business can be an exciting yet terrifying experience. While the enthusiasm for creating something new can be compelling, the vast unknowns can be overwhelming. For this reason, a well-crafted business plan is essential to the success of any new venture. In addition, a good business plan helps guide the startup process and provides a blueprint for future growth and development. This chapter will discuss the steps necessary to create a successful business plan.

1. Research and Define Your Business Vision

Before you can start writing a business plan, it's essential to understand your business's vision. This requires researching and defining your business idea, target audience, and unique selling proposition. Some questions to ask yourself as you explore your business idea are:

- What problem does my business solve?
- Who are my target customers?
- Who are my competitors?
- What makes my business unique?

Once you clearly understand your business vision, you can create a comprehensive business plan.

2. Begin with an Executive Summary

The executive summary is a brief overview of your business plan, typically consisting of one or two pages. This section should include an overview of your business, its mission, and its objectives. It should also include a summary of your financial projections and a brief description of the products or services that you will offer.

3. Identify Your Market

Understanding your target market is essential to the success of your business. This includes identifying and analyzing your competition and defining your unique value proposition. To do this, conduct market research to identify your target customers and their needs. Then, determine your competitors' strengths and weaknesses and find ways to differentiate your business from theirs.

4. Develop Your Marketing Strategy

Your marketing strategy should be based on the research conducted in the previous step. Next, determine how to reach your target audience and what channels you will use to communicate with them. Finally, consider the budget required to execute your marketing plan and ensure it aligns with your financial projections.

5. Create a Financial Plan

The financial plan is crucial to your business plan, outlining your revenue, expenses, and cash flow projections. This section should include your startup costs, monthly costs, and sales projections. Be sure to include a break-even analysis, which will help you determine the point at which your business will start to make a profit.

6. Define Your Organizational Structure

The organizational structure outlines how your business will be structured, including the roles and responsibilities of each team member. Consider the management structure, the leadership team, and any advisors or mentors you will work with. Determine who will be responsible for each aspect of the business, such as marketing, sales, and operations.

7. Determine Your Funding Needs

Depending on the type of business you are starting, you may need to secure funding to get your business off the ground or fuel growth. This section should outline your funding needs, including the amount of capital required and the funding sources, such as loans or investments from partners.

8. Evaluate Risk and Develop a Contingency Plan

Every business plan must incorporate a contingency plan to deal with unexpected events or risks that could derail your business. First, identify the significant risks to your business, such as market changes or supply chain disruptions. Then, develop contingency plans to mitigate those risks, such as finding alternative suppliers or diversifying your product line.

9. Continually Update and Refine Your Plan

Creating a business plan is an ongoing process. Your business plan should be updated regularly to reflect changes in the market or shifts in your business strategy. Continually refining your plan will ensure that your business stays on track and remains aligned with your long-term goals.

Following the steps outlined above, you can create a comprehensive plan to guide your startup process and help you achieve your business goals. Remember that a business plan is a living document that should be updated regularly to reflect changes in the market or shifts in your business strategy. Continually refining your plan will increase your chances of success and build a thriving business over time.

Chapter Three
Market Research: Understanding Your Competition and Niche

Market research is a critical aspect of any business strategy. Understanding your competition and niche makes it easier to make informed decisions about the direction and growth of your business. This chapter will explore the importance of market research and how it can help you gain a competitive advantage.

Understanding Your Competition

One of the primary reasons for conducting market research is to gain insights into your competition. Knowing who your competitors are, what they offer, and their strengths and weaknesses can provide valuable information that can be leveraged to gain a competitive advantage. Here are some of the key ways in which market research helps you understand your competition.

Identifying Competitors

The first step in understanding your competition is to identify who they are. This involves researching companies that offer products or services that are similar to yours. You can use online directories, industry publications, and social media platforms to identify competitors. Once you have a list of competitors, you can start collecting information about them.

Analyzing Competitor Strategies

Once you have identified your competitors, the next step is to analyze their strategies. This involves researching their pricing, marketing, and distribution channels. You can use online tools such as SEMrush or Ahrefs to gather information about your competitors' digital marketing strategies. You can also use tools such as SimilarWeb to analyze their website traffic and social media activity.

Understanding Competitor Strengths and Weaknesses

You can gain insights into your competitors' strengths and weaknesses by analyzing their strategies. This can help you identify areas where you can differentiate and offer more value to your customers. For example, if your competitors are not offering a particular feature or service, you can consider offering it to differentiate yourself in the market.

Studying Customer Reviews

Customer reviews can provide valuable insights into your competitors' products or services. You can identify areas where your competitors are excelling or falling short by reading customer reviews on sites like Yelp or Google My Business; you can identify areas where your competitors are excelling or falling short. This can help you identify opportunities to improve your products or services and meet your customers' needs.

Understanding Your Niche

In addition to understanding your competition, market research can also help you know your niche. A niche is a specific market segment that shares similar needs or characteristics. Understanding your niche is important because it enables you to tailor your products or services to meet the needs of your target audience better. Here are some of the key ways in which market research can help you understand your niche.

Identifying Customer Needs

One of the primary goals of market research is to identify customer needs. You can gain insights into your target audience's pain points and challenges by conducting surveys, focus groups, or online research.

14

This can help you identify opportunities to develop products or services that better meet their needs.

Segmenting Your Market

Once you have identified your target audience's needs, you can start segmenting your market. This involves dividing your target audience into smaller groups based on similar characteristics or needs. For example, if you offer a software tool for project management, you can segment your market into small business owners, freelance professionals, and enterprise clients.

Developing Customer Personas

Customer personas are fictional representations of your target audience. By creating customer personas, you can better understand your target audience's motivations, pain points, and behavior patterns. This can help you tailor your marketing messages and product offerings to resonate better with your audience.

Developing Your Unique Value Proposition

Understanding your niche allows you to develop a unique value proposition that differentiates you from your competitors. A value proposition is a statement that communicates your product or service's unique benefits and value to your target audience. You can better attract and retain customers by developing a solid value proposition.

Market research is a vital component of any successful business strategy. By understanding your competition and niche, you can identify opportunities to differentiate and gain a competitive advantage. Whether launching a new product or looking to grow your business, market research can provide valuable insights to help you make informed decisions and achieve your goals.

Chapter Four
Finding Your Target Audience and Creating a Customer Persona

As a business owner, you want to create a message that resonates with your customers. That message must speak to their needs, desires, and pain points. But how do you create a message that speaks to your customers and converts them into buyers? The answer lies in finding your target audience and creating a customer persona.

What is a Target Audience?

A target audience is the individuals most likely to be interested in your product or service. To find your target audience, you must begin by researching and analyzing your ideal customer.

How to Identify Your Target Audience

1. Define Your Product or Service

The first step in identifying your target audience is to define your product or service. Next, you must understand your product's unique features, benefits, and purpose. What makes your product special? How does it solve your customer's problems? By answering these questions, you can begin to understand who your customers are.

2. Analyze Your Competition

Your competition can be a great source of information when identifying your target audience. First, find out whom they are targeting and what messaging they use. This information can help you refine your messaging and identify which customers you want to target.

3. Conduct Market Research

Market research is an essential step in identifying your target audience. You can use surveys, focus groups, and other research methods to gather information about your potential customers. Ask questions about their demographics, interests, and buying habits.

4. Analyze Your Current Customers

Your current customers can provide valuable insights into your target audience. First, analyze their demographics, buying habits, and interests.

5. Create a Customer Persona

Once you have gathered all the necessary data, you can create a customer persona. A customer persona is a representation of your ideal customer. It includes their demographics, interests, pain points, and buying behavior. Creating a customer persona helps you understand your customers on a deeper level and create messaging that speaks to them.

Tips for Creating a Customer Persona

1. Use Real Data

Your customer persona should be based on real data, not assumptions or guesses. Therefore, gather as much data as possible to represent your ideal customer accurately.

2. Use Personas to Guide Your Marketing Strategy

Customer personas should guide your marketing strategy, messaging, and content creation. Use them to ensure you are creating content that speaks to your customers' needs and desires.

3. Don't Overcomplicate It

Creating a customer persona can be simple. But first, focus on the most important characteristics that define your ideal customer.

4. Revise Your Persona Over Time

Your customer persona is not set in stone. Revise it over time as you gather more data and your customers change.

Finding your target audience and creating a customer persona is critical for any business looking to develop messaging that speaks to its customers. By identifying your ideal customer and understanding their needs and desires, you can create a marketing strategy that resonates with them and converts them into buyers. Remember to use real data, use personas to guide your marketing strategy, keep it simple, and revise your persona over time.

Chapter Five
Branding Your Startup: Creating a Memorable Identity

In today's fast-paced business world, startups are popping up left and right. With so many companies vying for attention, startups must establish a strong brand identity that sets them apart from the competition. In this chapter, we'll explore the importance of branding your startup and how you can create a memorable identity that resonates with your target audience.

Why is branding important for startups?

Branding is vital for any business, but it's especially important for startups trying to establish themselves in a crowded marketplace. A strong brand identity helps your startup to stand out from the competition, establish trust with potential customers, and create a sense of loyalty among current customers.

Branding also plays a significant role in shaping how people perceive your startup. Your brand is more than just a logo or a tagline; it's how people feel when they think about your company. A well-designed brand identity can evoke positive emotions and create a lasting impression in people's minds.

21

Creating a memorable identity for your startup

So how do you go about creating a memorable identity for your startup? Here are a few key steps to get started:

1. Define your brand values

Before creating a brand identity, you need to define your brand values. What does your startup stand for? What are your core values? What sets you apart from the competition? These are all questions you need to answer before you can start to develop your brand.

To define your brand values, start by considering your mission statement. For example, what is the purpose of your startup, and what do you hope to achieve? From there, you can develop a set of core values that align with your mission and guide your company's actions.

2. Develop a brand personality

Your brand personality is the set of characteristics that define your brand's voice, tone, and style. It's how your brand comes across to your audience and the personality traits it embodies.

To develop your brand personality, consider your target audience. What kind of personality traits do they find appealing? For example, are they looking for a fun and lighthearted brand or prefer a more serious and professional tone? Once you've identified your target audience, you can develop a brand personality that resonates with them.

3. Create a memorable logo

Your logo is the visual representation of your brand identity, one of the most important elements of your branding strategy. A well-designed logo makes a strong first impression and sets the tone for your brand identity.

To create a memorable logo, consider your brand values and personality. What visual elements best represent your brand? What colors and fonts align with your brand personality? From there, you can work with a graphic designer to create a logo that captures the essence of your brand.

4. Develop a consistent brand voice and tone

Consistency is key when it comes to branding. Your brand voice and tone should be consistent across all marketing materials, from your website to social media posts.

Develop guidelines that outline your brand's voice and tone to ensure consistency. These guidelines should include writing style, language usage, and visual branding elements.

5. Create a strong brand story

A strong brand story can establish an emotional connection with your audience and create a sense of loyalty among your customers. Your brand story should explain why your startup exists, what problems you're solving, and how your products or services can help your target audience.

To create a strong brand story, consider what inspired you to start your startup in the first place. What challenges did you face, and how did you overcome them? From there, you can develop a narrative that resonates with your target audience and helps to establish your brand identity.

Branding your startup is a challenging feat. However, with the right strategy and a solid understanding of your brand values and personality, you can create a memorable identity that sets you apart from the competition.

Chapter Six
Creating a Solid Marketing Strategy

A marketing strategy is a plan of action implemented by an organization to promote its products or services to a target audience. By creating a solid marketing strategy, a company can quickly identify its potential customers, understand their needs, and develop promotional activities to satisfy those needs. It helps businesses to differentiate themselves from their competitors, communicate their unique value proposition, and achieve their sales goals.

Creating a marketing strategy can be challenging for a new business owner. Nevertheless, it is vital as it serves as a roadmap for achieving a company's marketing goals and objectives and aligns with the overall business strategy. The following are the essential steps to creating a successful marketing strategy.

1. Define Your Target Audience

Defining your target audience is the foundation of your marketing strategy. Your target audience is the group of people whom you want to reach with your products or services. Therefore, you need to know your target audience to create marketing messages that resonate with them.

To define your target audience, consider demographics, psychographics, and behavior. Demographics include age, gender, income, education, and occupation. Psychographics include values, attitudes, interests, and lifestyle. Finally, behavior includes buying habits, preferences, and decision-making patterns.

2. Set Your Marketing Goals and Objectives

Once you have defined your target audience, setting your marketing goals and objectives is the next step. Your marketing goals should be specific, measurable, achievable, relevant, and time-bound. In addition, they should be aligned with your overall business strategy and vision.

Your marketing objectives should be based on your business goals. For example, if you want to increase sales, your marketing objective might be to generate more leads or increase website traffic. To build brand awareness, your marketing objective might be to increase social media engagement or improve your search engine rankings.

3. Understand Your Competitive Landscape

Understanding your competitive landscape is critical to developing a successful marketing strategy. You need to know who your competitors are, what they offer, and how they promote their products or services. This information will help you identify your unique selling proposition and develop strategies to differentiate yourself from your competitors.

4. Develop Your Unique Value Proposition

Your unique value proposition (UVP) sets you apart from your competitors. It is why customers should buy from you instead of your competitors. Your UVP should be clear, concise, and easy to understand. It should focus on your products or services' benefits to your target audience.

5. Develop Your Marketing Mix

Your marketing mix is the combination of tactics that you will use to promote your products or services. The four Ps of marketing – product, price, promotion, and place – should be considered when developing your marketing mix.

Product: Your product should meet the needs of your target audience. It should be unique, high quality, and provide value to your customers.

Price: Your pricing strategy should be based on your target audience and competitors. It should be competitive and reflect your product or service's value.

Promotion: Your promotional tactics should be based on your marketing goals and objectives. They should include online and offline marketing activities such as social media, email marketing, content marketing, events, and advertising.

Place: Your distribution strategy should be based on your target audience and marketing goals. Consider where your target audience spends their time and how they prefer to buy products or services.

6. Develop a Budget and Implementation Plan

Developing a budget and implementation plan is critical to achieving your marketing goals and objectives. Your budget should include all the costs associated with your marketing tactics, such as advertising, content creation, social media management, and event planning.

Your implementation plan should include a timeline and a list of tasks that need to be completed to execute your marketing tactics successfully. It should also include metrics that you will use to measure the effectiveness of your marketing activities.

7. Evaluate and Measure Your Results

The final step in creating a successful marketing strategy is evaluating and measuring your results. You need to track and analyze the effectiveness of your marketing tactics to determine what is working and what is not. You can use metrics such as website traffic, social media engagement, lead generation, and sales to measure the effectiveness of your marketing activities.

Creating a solid marketing strategy is essential for any business to achieve its marketing goals and objectives. It involves defining your target audience, setting your marketing goals and objectives, understanding your competitive landscape, developing your unique value proposition and marketing mix, developing a budget and implementation plan, and evaluating and measuring your results.

Chapter Seven
Designing a Great Logo and Website

In today's digital age, it's imperative for businesses to have an online presence to reach their target audience. One of the most important aspects of establishing an online presence is having a great logo and website representing your brand identity. In addition, a well-designed logo and website can create an immediate impression on visitors and make them want to explore your business further. This chapter will dive into the critical elements of designing a great logo and website.

Designing a Great Logo

Your logo is often the first visual representation of your business that people see, so it must convey what you're about. A great logo should be memorable, timeless, and able to represent your brand without words. Here are some key elements to keep in mind when designing a great logo:

Simplicity - The simpler the logo design, the easier it is for people to remember it. A cluttered or overly complex logo can be confusing, and people may need help recalling it later.

Color - The colors you choose for your logo can significantly impact its perception. Colors can evoke emotions and be associated with industries, so choose carefully.

Typography - The font you choose for your logo can also impact how it's perceived. Consider using a font that aligns with your brand's personality and conveys the right tone.

Scalability - Your logo should be designed to work across various mediums and sizes. It should be legible, recognizable in small sizes, and look great blown up on signage or billboards.

Here are some examples of great logos:

- Nike: The swoosh is simple, recognizable, and memorable. The logo represents movement and athleticism, which aligns perfectly with Nike's brand identity.

- Apple: The iconic Apple logo is simple, timeless, and represents the brand's innovation and creativity.

- FedEx: The negative space between the "E" and "X" creates an arrow representing speed and movement. It's a clever and memorable logo design.

Designing a Great Website

Once you've established a great logo, the next step is creating a website that aligns with your brand identity and goals. Here are some key elements to keep in mind when designing a great website:

Consistency - Your website design should be consistent with your brand's visual identity, including typography, color palette, and imagery. This consistency helps build brand recognition and trust with visitors.

User Experience - Your website should be easy to navigate, intuitive, and provide a seamless user experience. This means using clear navigation menus, easily accessible information, and logical page layouts.

Mobile-Responsive - With more and more people accessing the internet on their mobile devices, having a mobile-responsive website is crucial. This means designing a site that adapts to different screen sizes and is easily used on a mobile device.

Loading Speed - A slow-loading website can frustrate visitors and negatively impact your search engine rankings. Your website should load quickly, especially on mobile devices.

Content - Your website's content should be clear, concise, and engaging. It should give visitors the information they want while aligning with your brand's voice and personality.

Here are some examples of great websites:

- Airbnb: Airbnb's website design is clean, visually appealing, and mobile-responsive. The imagery and typography align with the brand's personality, making the user experience seamless.

- Squarespace: Squarespace's website design is simple and elegant, focusing on visual content. The user experience is intuitive, with clear navigation menus and easily accessible information.

- Dropbox: Dropbox's website design is minimalistic, with bright colors and bold typography. The site loads quickly and is easy to use on mobile devices.

In conclusion, designing a great logo and website is crucial for building a strong online presence and establishing a strong brand identity. Keeping key elements such as simplicity, color, typography, consistency, user experience, mobile responsiveness, loading speed, and content in mind, you can create a logo and website that aligns with your brand's personality, goals, and goals values.

Chapter Eight
Funding Your Startup: The Different Options

Starting a new business is an exciting journey. However, it can become difficult and frustrating without proper funding. There are various options available for aspiring entrepreneurs to fund their startups, all of which have advantages and disadvantages. This chapter will discuss the different funding options available to help you decide which one suits your needs.

Bootstrapping

Bootstrapping is one of the most popular funding options amongst entrepreneurs. Bootstrapping entails using personal savings, credit cards, and existing resources to start and grow your business. The most significant advantage of bootstrapping is maintaining complete control of your business. You don't have to seek approval from investors or worry about diluting your equity. Furthermore, it lets you keep costs low, which is crucial when starting a new business.

However, bootstrapping also has its downsides. It limits the amount of money available for expansion and scaling up the business. It also places a lot of pressure on the entrepreneur, who must work hard to earn enough money to sustain the business. Therefore, bootstrapping may be ideal for small businesses that do not require massive amounts of funding.

Crowdfunding

Crowdfunding is rapidly becoming a popular way of funding new businesses. It involves getting small amounts of money from many people to fund your startup. Crowdfunding platforms such as Kickstarter and Indiegogo allow businesses to pitch their ideas to a large audience and raise funds from supporters who believe in their vision. Crowdfunding enables entrepreneurs to access much-needed capital and test the viability of their idea before bringing it to market.

Crowdfunding can also generate useful feedback from potential customers, which can help to refine the business idea. However, one of the significant disadvantages of crowdfunding is that there are no guarantees that a campaign will be successful. Crowdfunding campaigns require a lot of time and effort to create and promote, and even if the campaign is successful, more than the funds raised may be needed to support the business's growth.

Angel Investors

Angel investors are wealthy individuals who invest in startups in exchange for equity or ownership in the company. They typically invest in businesses in the early stages of development and provide the funds needed to get the business off the ground. Angel investors also bring their experience and networks to the table, which can be valuable in helping the business grow.

Angel investors have a higher risk tolerance than traditional lenders, making them more likely to invest in risky ventures. In addition, they are often more flexible than traditional lenders, allowing for more favorable terms. However, angel investors usually expect a significant return on their investment, which can take time to achieve. In addition, they may require considerable equity in the business, diluting the founder's ownership.

Venture Capital

Venture capital (VC) funding involves raising money from institutional investors with large amounts to invest in high-growth, high-potential businesses. Venture capital firms are looking for businesses that have the potential to generate significant returns. They invest in businesses in the early stages of development, and their primary goal is to provide the funding needed to help the business grow quickly.

VC funding has many advantages, including access to significant amounts of capital and the expertise and networks of venture capitalists. They can also provide valuable mentorship and advice to help the business grow. However, VC firms typically require a significant amount of equity in the business, which can dilute the founder's ownership. They also have a high threshold for success and may push the business to make decisions that prioritize short-term growth over long-term profitability.

Bank Loans

Bank loans are the most traditional form of funding for businesses. They involve borrowing money from a bank or financial institution and repaying it over time with interest. Bank loans typically offer lower interest rates than other forms of funding. As a result, they are often available to businesses with a solid credit history and track record of generating revenue.

Bank loans also have their disadvantages. The application process can be long and arduous, often requiring significant collateral to secure the loan. Moreover, banks may require personal guarantees from the business owner, putting their personal assets at risk.

When starting a new business, choosing the right funding option is crucial. Each funding option has advantages and disadvantages; entrepreneurs must weigh these carefully before deciding.

Chapter Nine
Creating an Effective Pitch Deck

A compelling pitch deck is crucial when securing funding for a project or business. This visual presentation outlines your business or idea to potential investors or lenders. It should be engaging, informative, and persuasive. In this chapter, we will discuss the key elements of a pitch deck and how to create an effective one.

1. Start with a strong opening

The very first slide of your pitch deck should grab your audience's attention. If you don't capture their attention in the first few seconds, they may tune out for the rest of the presentation. So start with a compelling headline and a clear value proposition. This should clearly describe your project or business and what makes it unique.

2. Tell a story

A pitch deck is not just a collection of facts and figures. It's a story that should engage your audience and get them excited about your project. Focus on the problem or need your project addresses and how your solution will solve it. Use anecdotes or case studies to illustrate your points.

3. Keep it concise

The ideal length for a pitch deck is 10 to 12 slides. This means you need to be selective with information. Avoid going into too much detail, and keep things simple. Use infographics or charts to present data in a visually appealing way.

4. Know your audience

Before you start creating your pitch deck, you need to understand who your audience will be. For example, if you're presenting to a group of venture capitalists, you'll need to emphasize the potential return on investment. If you're presenting to a group of potential customers, on the other hand, you'll need to focus on the benefits of your product or service.

5. Be clear about your business model

Your pitch deck should clearly outline how your project or business will make money. Explain your revenue streams, your pricing strategy, and your target market. Be realistic and avoid making grandiose claims. You need to demonstrate that you have a solid understanding of your industry and your competitors.

6. Showcase your team

Investors are not just investing in your project; they're investing in your team. Make sure you highlight the experience and expertise of your key team members. Explain their roles and how they fit into the overall project. If you have any advisors or mentors, include them as well.

7. Highlight your achievements

If you've already achieved some milestones, such as securing your first customers or launching a prototype, highlight them in your pitch deck. This shows that you're making progress and that you're capable of executing your plan.

8. Include a call to action

Include a clear call to action at the end of your pitch deck. For example, what do you want your audience to do next? Are you looking for funding? Are you looking for partnerships or collaborations? Ensure you provide clear contact information and follow up with potential investors or partners after the presentation.

9. Practice, practice, practice

Finally, practicing your pitch is essential. You need to be comfortable with your material and able to deliver it confidently. Time yourself and ensure you can deliver your pitch within the allotted time. You should also be prepared to answer any questions your audience might have.

Creating an effective pitch deck requires careful planning, concise messaging, and a well-organized presentation. By following these tips, you can create a powerful pitch deck that engages your audience and helps secure the funding or partnerships you need to bring your project to life.

Chapter Ten
Building a Strong Team: Hiring and Management

An organization's success is directly linked to the strength of its team. A team with strong leadership, communication, and collaboration skills can achieve more than individuals working alone. However, building a strong team is a challenging task. It requires a combination of effective hiring practices and management strategies to ensure that the right people are in the right roles and working together efficiently.

Hiring the Right People

Hiring the right people is the first step toward building a strong team. But how do you know who the right people are? Here are some tips for finding candidates who will be a good fit for your team:

Define the Job Role Clearly:
Before posting a job, ensure you have a clear idea of what the role entails, including the skills required and any specific qualifications or experience needed.

Advertise in the Right Places:
To attract suitable candidates, you need to advertise the job in the places where they are most likely to look. This might include job boards, social media, or industry-specific sites.

Screen Resumes Carefully:
Use the job description to screen resumes carefully and choose only those candidates who meet the specific requirements of the role.

Conduct Effective Interviews:
Interviews are a chance to get to know the candidate better and assess their suitability for the role. Use behavioral and situational questions to understand how they might perform on the job.

Check References:
Always check references before making an offer to ensure that the candidate has the experience and skills they claim to have.

Assess Cultural Fit:
Finally, assess the candidate's cultural fit with your organization. This means considering their values, communication style, and work ethic to ensure they will fit well within your team.

Managing the Team Effectively

Once you have hired the right people, the next step is to manage them effectively. Effective management is essential for building a strong team working together efficiently and achieving the organization's goals. Here are some tips for managing your team effectively:

Set Clear Expectations:
Make sure that everyone on the team understands what is expected of them, both in terms of their individual and overall team goals.

Communicate Effectively:
Communication is key to building a strong team. Ensure that everyone is clear on what is happening, their role, and how they can contribute to the team's success.

Provide Feedback:
Regular feedback is essential for helping team members improve and stay motivated. Make sure to provide both positive feedback and constructive criticism in a timely manner.

Encourage Collaboration:
Encourage team members to collaborate and work together to achieve the team's goals. This might involve breaking down silos between departments or creating cross-functional teams to tackle specific projects.

Recognize Achievements:
Celebrate team achievements and milestones to boost morale and motivation. This might involve something as simple as a public acknowledgment or a team outing to celebrate a successful project.

Address Conflicts:
Conflicts can arise in any team, and addressing them quickly and effectively is essential. Encourage open communication and work with team members to find a solution for everyone.

Provide Training and Development:
Finally, ensure training and development opportunities for team members to continue to grow and develop in their roles. This might involve providing access to courses or workshops or assigning a mentor to guide them through their career.

Measuring Success

Measuring your team's success is essential for understanding what works well and what needs improvement. There are several key metrics that you can use to measure the success of your team:

Productivity:
Productivity measures how much work the team can complete within a given timeframe. This might include

the number of projects completed or the revenue generated.

Quality:
Quality measures how well the team can complete work to a high standard. This might include customer satisfaction ratings or the number of errors or defects in a product.

Employee Satisfaction:
Employee satisfaction measures how happy and motivated team members are. This might include surveys, feedback sessions, or retention rates.

Collaboration:
Collaboration measures how well team members work together to achieve their goals. This might involve assessing how well individuals are communicating and collaborating on projects.

Building a solid team is essential for the success of any organization. It requires a combination of effective hiring practices and management strategies to ensure that the right people are in the right roles and working together efficiently. Managers can create a culture of collaboration and continuous improvement by setting clear expectations, communicating effectively, providing regular feedback, and recognizing achievements.

Chapter Eleven
Legal Considerations: Protecting Your Intellectual Property

Intellectual property (IP) is a legal term that refers to creations of the mind, such as inventions, literary and artistic works, symbols, names, and designs. It is a valuable asset for businesses and individuals and protecting it is essential to safeguard their rights and interests. Intellectual property rights (IPRs) refer to the exclusive legal rights granted to the creators and owners of IP to use, sell, or license their ideas, creativity, and innovation. This chapter will discuss the legal considerations for protecting your intellectual property.

Types of Intellectual Property

Businesses and individuals need to protect several types of intellectual property. They include:

1. Patents:
A patent is a legal document that grants an inventor the exclusive right to make, use, and sell their invention for a specified period. The government grants it in exchange for the disclosure of the invention to the public.

2. Trademarks:
A trademark is a symbol, word, or phrase used to

distinguish a company's products or services from those of others.

3. Copyrights:
A copyright is a legal protection that gives the creator of a work exclusive rights to use and distribute it.

4. Trade secrets:
A trade secret is confidential information that provides a company with a competitive advantage, such as customer lists, manufacturing processes, and formulas.

Legal Considerations for Protecting Your Intellectual Property

1. Register Your Intellectual Property:
The first step to protecting your intellectual property is to register it with the relevant government agency. For example, you can register with the United States Patent and Trademark Office (USPTO) for patents. Likewise, you can register trademarks with the USPTO or the state government. For copyrights, you automatically get protection once you create the work, but you can also register with the US Copyright Office to strengthen your legal rights.

2. Conduct a Trademark Search:
Before registering your trademark, it's important to conduct a trademark search to ensure that no one else

uses a similar mark. This can prevent costly legal disputes down the road.

3. Use Non-Disclosure Agreements:

If you have trade secrets that you want to protect, you should use non-disclosure agreements (NDAs) with employees, contractors, and partners. An NDA is a legal contract prohibiting the recipient from disclosing confidential information to third parties.

4. Monitor Your Intellectual Property:

Once you have registered your intellectual property, you should monitor it for unauthorized use. You can use online tools such as Google Alerts and social media monitoring to keep track of your trademarks and copyrights.

5. Enforce Your Intellectual Property Rights:

If someone infringes on your intellectual property rights, you have the legal right to take action. This can include cease and desist letters, injunctions, and lawsuits. Again, working with an experienced intellectual property attorney is important to protect your rights.

6. Use Contracts and Licenses:

If you want to license your intellectual property to others, it's crucial to use contracts that clearly define the terms of the agreement. This can include the duration of the license, the rights granted, and the payment terms.

7. Protect Your IP Internationally:
If you do business internationally, protecting your intellectual property in other countries is vital. This can include registering your trademark or patent in other countries and working with local attorneys to enforce your rights.

The Importance of Protecting Your Intellectual Property

Protecting your intellectual property is essential for several reasons:

1. It can protect your competitive advantage:
If you have a patented product or a trademarked brand, you have a competitive advantage. Protecting your intellectual property can prevent others from copying your ideas and taking away your market share.

2. It can increase your company's value:
Intellectual property can be a valuable asset for a company. Strong trademarks, patents, and copyrights can increase your company's value in the eyes of investors and potential buyers.

3. It can prevent costly legal disputes:
If someone infringes on your intellectual property rights, it can lead to expensive legal disputes. By protecting your intellectual property, you can prevent these

disputes from happening or have a stronger legal case if they do.

Legal considerations for protecting your intellectual property include registering your IP, conducting trademark searches, using NDAs, monitoring for unauthorized use, enforcing your rights, using contracts and licenses, and protecting your IP internationally.

Chapter Twelve
Choosing the Right Business Structure

Starting a business can be a challenging experience. One of the most important decisions that an entrepreneur will have to make is the choice of business structure. The chosen structure will significantly impact how the business operates, its legal and financial obligations, and the level of control the owner will have over the business.

Several business structures include sole proprietorship, partnership, limited liability company (LLC), and corporation. Each structure has advantages and disadvantages, and the choice depends on several factors, such as the type of business, size, ownership, and financial goals.

Sole Proprietorship

A sole proprietorship is the most common form of business structure. It is an unincorporated business that is owned and operated by one person. This structure is simple and requires minimal paperwork and legal formalities. The owner controls the business and receives all profits and losses.

One of the main disadvantages of a sole proprietorship is that the owner is personally liable for all debts and legal issues that arise from the business. This means that if the business is sued, the owner's personal assets may be at risk.

Partnership

Conversely, a partnership involves two or more individuals who share ownership, profits, and losses. All partners have unlimited personal liability for business debts and obligations in a general partnership. This means that partners are personally liable for any legal or financial issues that arise from the business.

It is essential to have a partnership agreement that outlines the responsibilities and rights of each partner, including profit distribution, decision-making, and how the business will be managed.

Limited Partnership

Limited partnerships (LPs) are partnerships that have both general partners and limited partners. General partners manage the business and are personally liable for its debts and obligations. In contrast, limited partners are passive investors who contribute capital but have little involvement in day-to-day operations. As a result, they have limited liability and are not personally responsible for business debts and liabilities.

Limited Liability Company (LLC)

A limited liability company (LLC) is a hybrid structure that offers the benefits of both a partnership and a corporation. In addition, this structure provides the owners with limited liability protection, meaning that they are not personally responsible for the debts and obligations of the business.

An LLC is a popular choice for small businesses, as it is relatively easy to set up and requires minimal paperwork. It also offers flexibility in terms of management and taxation. For example, owners can be taxed as a partnership or a corporation.

Corporation

A corporation is a separate legal entity that can own property, enter into contracts, and sue or be sued. It is owned by shareholders who elect a board of directors to manage the business. Shareholders have limited liability protection and are only responsible for the amount of money invested in the company.

One of the main advantages of a corporation is that it can raise capital by issuing stocks and bonds. However, it is subject to double taxation – the corporation pays taxes on its profits, and shareholders pay taxes on the dividends they receive.

Choosing the proper business structure depends on several factors, such as the nature of the business, the number of owners, and the level of liability protection required. Here are some of the critical factors to consider:

Liability Protection

Liability protection is a critical consideration when choosing a business structure. For example, sole proprietors and general partners in a partnership have unlimited personal liability, which means their personal assets may be at risk if the business is sued or goes bankrupt.

Limited partners have limited liability, while LLC owners and shareholders in a corporation have limited liability protection, which means that their personal assets are not at risk if the business is sued or goes bankrupt.

Taxation

Taxation is another essential factor to consider when choosing a business structure. Sole proprietors and general partners pay taxes on the business profits as personal income. LLCs and partnerships are pass-through entities, meaning the business profits and losses are passed through to the owners' personal tax returns.

Corporations are taxed as separate entities, and shareholders pay taxes on their dividends. This means that corporations are subject to double taxation.

Management

The management structure is another important factor to consider. Sole proprietors have complete control over the business, while partners share management responsibilities. LLCs and corporations have a more formal management structure, with managers and directors overseeing the day-to-day operations.

Flexibility

Flexibility is another factor to consider when choosing a business structure. For example, sole proprietorships and partnerships are flexible and require minimal legal formalities. On the other hand, LLCs and corporations have more formal requirements, such as maintaining minutes of meetings and filing annual reports.

Choosing the proper business structure is crucial for the success of any business. However, each structure has advantages and disadvantages, and the choice depends on several factors, such as the type of business, ownership, and financial goals. Therefore, seeking professional advice and considering all the elements is essential before deciding.

Chapter Thirteen
Navigating Tax and Regulatory Compliance

Navigating tax and regulatory compliance can be daunting for businesses of any size. From registering with the appropriate licensing authorities to filing taxes on time, businesses must adhere to many regulations to avoid fines, penalties, and legal action. Tax and regulatory compliance can also be costly and time-consuming, hindering business growth and profitability. However, compliance is necessary to protect a business's legal and financial well-being and to ensure that it operates ethically and within the bounds of the law.

One of the first steps a business must take to comply with tax and regulatory requirements is to register with the relevant licensing authorities. This may include obtaining a business license, registering for an Employer Identification Number (EIN), and obtaining any necessary permits or certifications for the industry or location in which the business operates. Failure to register with the appropriate authorities can result in legal action and fines, so it's important to ensure that all necessary registrations are completed early.

In addition to licensing, businesses must also comply with tax regulations. This entails filing annual tax returns, paying taxes on time, and collecting and remitting sales tax (if applicable) and payroll taxes for any employees. It may also involve maintaining accurate financial records and providing them to tax authorities upon request. Failure to comply with tax regulations can result in significant financial penalties, interest charges, and even criminal charges in some cases.

Navigating regulatory compliance can also include complying with industry-specific regulations. For example, businesses that operate in the healthcare or financial industries may be subject to specific regulations governing data privacy, security, and compliance with federal and state regulations. These regulations may require additional certifications, training, and reporting to ensure that the business operates within the bounds of the law and industry-specific best practices.

Beyond these general compliance requirements, businesses must also pay attention to changing regulations and laws, which can impact tax and regulatory compliance. For example, changes to tax laws or regulations may require businesses to adjust their accounting practices or tax planning strategies. Similarly, changes in data privacy or security regulation may require companies to update their policies and procedures to remain compliant.

Given the complexity of navigating tax and regulatory compliance, many businesses hire professional advisors or consultants specializing in these areas. These individuals or firms can help businesses identify and navigate compliance requirements, provide guidance on best practices, and offer ongoing support to ensure the business remains compliant over time. This can be particularly helpful for businesses new to the regulatory landscape or those operating in multiple jurisdictions with varying compliance requirements.

Ultimately, navigating tax and regulatory compliance requires careful attention to detail, a strong understanding of relevant regulations and laws, and a commitment to operating ethically and within the bounds of the law. By taking these steps, businesses can protect themselves from fines, penalties, and legal action and ensure that they operate in a compliant, sustainable, and profitable way.

Chapter Fourteen
Scaling Your Business: Tips for Growth

As a business owner, one of your primary goals is to grow and scale your business. Scaling refers to increasing your business's size and revenue without compromising quality. However, scaling your business can be a daunting task, and many entrepreneurs need help with how to approach it. In this chapter, we will explore some tips for growth that will help you scale your business successfully.

1. Clarify your vision and set your goals

Before scaling your business, you must envision what you want to achieve. Next, define your goals and identify what actions you need to take to reach them. This process will help you create a roadmap for your business's growth and ensure your efforts align with your vision.

2. Focus on your core competencies

One of the most common mistakes businesses make is trying to do too much too soon. When scaling your business, you must focus on your core competencies and prioritize your efforts. Identify what your business does best and make it your focus. This will help you stay focused and deliver your customers the best product or service.

3. Build a strong team

A strong team is significantly critical to any business's success when scaling. As your business grows, you will need more talented people to handle the increased workload. Be sure to hire people who are passionate about your vision and have the skills and experience to help you achieve your goals. Train your employees and empower them to take ownership of their roles. This will help you build a strong team committed to your business's success.

4. Automate your processes

Automation can help you scale your business by reducing the time and effort required to perform certain tasks. Identify repetitive tasks that can be automated, such as invoicing, order processing, and customer service. Automating these tasks will free up more time for you to focus on growing your business.

5. Use technology to your advantage

Technology can be a powerful tool for scaling your business. Use technology to streamline your processes, increase efficiency, and improve your customer experience. Invest in software and tools that can help you manage your business more effectively, such as customer relationship management (CRM) software, project management tools, and marketing automation software.

6. Expand your reach

To scale your business, you need to expand your reach and find new customers. Use social media, email marketing, and other digital marketing channels to reach new audiences. Attend trade shows and networking events to connect with other businesses in your industry. Look for opportunities to collaborate with other businesses to expand your reach and grow your customer base.

7. Manage your cash flow

Cash flow management is critical to any business's success, especially when scaling. Ensure you have a solid understanding of your financials and implement systems to manage your cash flow effectively. Monitor your expenses, track your revenue, and plan for future growth. Consider working with a financial advisor or accountant to help you manage your finances more effectively.

8. Be adaptable

As your business grows, you will inevitably encounter challenges and roadblocks. Therefore, it is important to be adaptable and willing to pivot your business when necessary. Be open to customer and employee feedback, and make changes as needed to improve your business's performance.

9. Stay focused on quality

As you scale your business, it is crucial to maintain the quality of your products or services. However, don't sacrifice quality for speed or volume. Instead, ensure that your products or services meet customers' needs and deliver value. Staying focused on quality will help you build a loyal customer base and differentiate your business from competitors.

Scaling your business can be challenging but essential to achieving long-term success. By clarifying your vision, focusing on your core competencies, building a solid team, automating your processes, using technology to your advantage, expanding your reach, managing your cash flow, being adaptable, and staying focused on quality, you can successfully scale your business and take it to the next level.

Chapter Fifteen
Managing Your Finances: Accounting and Budgeting

One of the most critical aspects of running a successful small business is the management of finances. Effective accounting and budgeting are essential components in keeping a business profitable, solvent, and growing. Proper accounting and budgeting practices help business owners make informed decisions, predict future expenses and income, and identify potential problems before they occur. This chapter will discuss the importance of accounting and budgeting for small businesses and provide tips for effectively managing your finances.

Accounting

Accounting is the process of recording and tracking financial transactions. It involves creating financial reports that accurately represent a company's financial status, such as balance sheets, income statements, and cash flow statements. Proper accounting practices help businesses keep track of their income and expenses, make informed decisions, and comply with tax laws and regulations.

There are two primary accounting methods: cash accounting and accrual accounting. Cash accounting records transactions when money is received or paid out. This simple and straightforward method makes it a popular choice for small businesses. However, it does not account for future expenses or revenue earned but has yet to be received.

Accrual accounting records transactions when they occur, regardless of when money is received or paid out. This method provides a more accurate picture of a company's financial status since it accounts for future expenses and revenue. However, it is more complex and requires greater skill and knowledge to implement effectively.

Small businesses can manage their accounting in several ways. One option is to do it themselves, using accounting software or spreadsheets. Another option is to hire an accountant or bookkeeper to manage their finances. Whichever option a business chooses, it is essential to maintain accurate records and stay up-to-date with tax laws and regulations.

Budgeting

Budgeting is creating a financial plan outlining a business's expected income and expenses over a specific period. Effective budgeting helps companies to plan for the future, identify potential problems, and allocate resources effectively.

To create a budget, businesses must identify fixed and variable expenses. Fixed expenses, such as rent or salaries, do not change monthly. Variable expenses, such as supplies or marketing, fluctuate based on various factors.

When creating a budget, it's essential to be realistic about income and expenses. If a business overestimates its revenue or underestimates its expenses, it can quickly run into financial trouble. Business owners should also consider unexpected expenses, such as repairs or legal fees, when creating a budget.

Once a budget is in place, monitoring actual income and expenses against the budget is critical. This helps businesses stay on track and make adjustments as necessary. It's also essential to review the budget periodically, as expenses and income can change over time.

Tips for Managing Your Finances

Managing finances can be overwhelming, even for experienced business owners. Here are a few tips to help small businesses effectively manage their finances:

1. Keep Accurate Records

Accurate record-keeping is the foundation of good financial management. Whether a business uses software or a manual system, keeping track of all financial transactions is essential. This includes sales, expenses, invoices, and receipts.

2. Separate Business and Personal Finances

One common mistake small business owners make is using personal funds to cover business expenses or vice versa. Keeping these finances separate is essential to avoid confusion and potential legal and tax issues.

3. Create a Contingency Fund

Unexpected expenses can arise at any time, so it's essential to have a contingency fund in place. This fund can help cover unexpected expenses or cash flow issues that arise.

4. Understand Tax Laws and Regulations

Tax laws and regulations are complex and can be challenging to navigate for small business owners. Therefore, it's vital to stay up-to-date with changes in tax laws and regulations and seek the advice of an accountant or tax professional if necessary.

5. Use Accounting and Budgeting Software

Accounting and budgeting software can help automate financial tasks, saving time and reducing the risk of errors. Many options are available, from simple spreadsheets to more complex software explicitly designed for small businesses.

Effective financial management is critical to the success of any small business. Proper accounting and budgeting practices help businesses make informed decisions, plan for the future, and avoid financial problems. By keeping accurate records, separating business and personal finances, creating a contingency fund, understanding tax laws and regulations, and using accounting and budgeting software, small business owners can effectively manage their finances and achieve long-term success.

Chapter Sixteen
Customer Acquisition and Retention Strategies

Customer acquisition and retention strategies are an integral part of any successful business. Acquisition strategies focus on attracting new customers, while retention strategies aim to keep existing customers loyal and satisfied. A successful business must balance both strategies to ensure long-term growth and profitability.

Customer Acquisition Strategies

1. Invest in Marketing:
One of the most effective ways to attract new customers is through marketing. There are various channels businesses can use to reach out to potential customers, such as social media, email marketing, print, radio, and television advertising.

2. Offer Promotions:
Offering discounts, free trials, or other promotions is a great way to attract new customers. Businesses can offer these promotions through their marketing channels or partner with other businesses to reach a wider audience.

3. Improve Customer Experience:
Providing exceptional customer service is another effective way to acquire new customers. Businesses prioritizing the customer experience tend to have more satisfied customers likelier to refer others to their business.

4. Leverage Referrals:
Encouraging existing customers to refer their friends and family to the business is a cost-effective way to acquire new customers. Businesses can offer referral incentives, such as discounts or free products/services.

5. Attend Events:
Trade shows, conferences, and networking events are another way to reach potential customers. Businesses can connect with other professionals in their industry and showcase their products/services to a targeted audience.

Customer Retention Strategies

1. Provide Excellent Customer Service:
Exceptional customer service is essential for customer retention. Businesses prioritizing customer service tend to have more satisfied customers who are likelier to stay loyal to the business.

2. Stay Connected:

Keeping in touch with customers through email marketing, social media, or other communication channels is key to retaining customers. Businesses can send updates, offers, or relevant information to keep customers engaged and interested in their products/services.

3. Offer Loyalty Programs:

Offering loyalty programs are a great way to keep customers returning. Businesses can offer rewards for repeat purchases, exclusive discounts, or other incentives to encourage customers to continue doing business with them.

4. Listen to Feedback:

Customer feedback is crucial for improving products/services and ensuring customer satisfaction. Businesses can ask for feedback through surveys, social media, or other channels to gain insights into what customers are looking for and how they can improve.

5. Personalize the Experience:

Personalizing the customer experience is another way to retain customers. Businesses can use data and analytics to understand customer preferences and tailor their products/services to meet their needs.

Chapter Seventeen
Business Networking: The Pros and Cons

Business networking is an essential part of the business world today. It is a platform for people to connect with other professionals in their industry and build relationships that can lead to new opportunities and growth. However, as with any tool, there are pros and cons to using business networking to advance one's career. In this chapter, we will look at the advantages and disadvantages of business networking.

Pros:

1. Opportunities for Growth: Networking opens doors to new opportunities, whether for jobs, partnerships, or collaborations. Meeting new people in your industry increases your chances of finding new opportunities that can help advance your career.

2. Building Connections: Networking is a great way to build connections with people in your industry. These connections can help you gain insights, share experiences, and provide the information you need to grow your business. The more people you connect with, the more benefits you can get from the connections.

3. Referral Business: One of the most significant benefits of networking is the referral business it can generate. When you connect with people in your industry, they can refer clients or customers to you, resulting in more business.

4. Thought Leadership: Networking allows you to showcase your expertise in your field. You can position yourself as a thought leader in your industry by sharing your insights and thoughts. This can lead to more speaking engagements, writing, or consulting opportunities.

5. Professional Development: Networking provides opportunities for learning and professional development. You can attend events, workshops, and conferences to learn from experts in your field and learn new skills to help you grow your career.

Cons:

1. Time-Consuming: Networking can be time-consuming, especially if you attend multiple events, conferences, and workshops. It can also be challenging to balance networking with other work responsibilities.

2. Cost: Networking can be costly, especially if you attend events or conferences that require registration

fees, travel, and accommodations. For people on a tight budget, the cost of networking can be prohibitive.

3. The Pressure to Network: Some people can feel immense pressure to network, leading to anxiety and stress. Remember that networking is not the only way to grow your career; there is no one-size-fits-all approach.

4. Information Overload: Social media networking makes it easy to feel overwhelmed by the amount of information being shared. It is essential to filter out the noise and focus on the information that is relevant and valuable to you.

5. Inauthentic Connections: Networking sometimes feels forced, leading to inauthentic connections. Building genuine and authentic relationships is essential for both parties to benefit from the connection.

Business networking can be an effective tool for growing one's career. The advantages of networking include opportunities for growth, building connections, referral business, thought leadership, and professional development. However, networking also has its cons, including being time-consuming, costly, pressure to network, information overload, and inauthentic connections. Therefore, it is essential to balance networking and other work responsibilities, filter out the noise, and build genuine connections that can benefit you and the other person.

Chapter Eighteen
Keeping Your Startup Relevant: Innovation and Adaptation

Starting a business is one thing, but keeping it relevant is another. In today's fast-paced, innovative economy, startup companies need to be able to adapt and change quickly to stay competitive. Innovation and adaptation are two crucial elements of keeping your startup relevant, and in this chapter, we will explore their importance and how you can employ them to ensure success.

The Importance of Innovation

Innovation is critical in today's business world because it sets you apart from your competition. It enables you to create new products, services, or processes that are more efficient, effective, or attractive to your target market. When you innovate, you stay ahead of the curve, and you can create a loyal customer base that appreciates the value you bring.

Innovation should be an ongoing process that is part of your business strategy. It does not necessarily mean that you need to develop something completely new; rather, it can be about improving what you already have.

For example, look at your products or services and examine where you can make changes to improve their quality, usability, or appeal.

You can also look at what your competition is doing and see if there is anything you can do better. This does not mean copying their ideas but instead using them as inspiration to create something original that will set you apart.

One way to encourage innovation is to foster a culture of creativity within your organization. First, encourage your team members to brainstorm and pitch ideas. Next, provide them with the necessary resources and support to develop and test new concepts. Finally, create a safe environment where failure is not punished but instead viewed as a learning opportunity.

The Importance of Adaptation

Adaptation is another critical element of keeping your startup relevant. As the market and customer needs change, you must adapt to these changes to stay competitive. This means you must be flexible and willing to change your business model, products, services, or processes as needed.

There are several ways you can adapt your startup to stay relevant. One approach is to keep up-to-date with industry trends and changes. This means you need to be aware of what is happening in your industry and how it may affect your business. Keeping up with industry news and attending conferences and events can help you stay informed.

Another way to adapt is to listen to your customers. Customer feedback is essential for improving your products, services, and processes. Regularly surveying your customers or soliciting feedback can help you identify improvement areas.

You can also adapt by being willing to pivot when necessary. If your current business model is not working, you need to be open to changing it. This could mean adding new products or services, targeting a different market, or changing your core values. Being willing to pivot can help you stay relevant when market conditions change.

Finally, being adaptable means being able to respond quickly to changes. This requires a level of agility in your business processes and decision-making. Having streamlined processes and an agile team can help you respond rapidly to new opportunities and challenges.

Innovation and Adaptation in Action

To see how innovation and adaptation can work together, let us consider the example of Netflix. When Netflix first started, it was a DVD-by-mail rental service. However, as technology changed, the company had to adapt to stay relevant. They saw the shift towards streaming services and decided to invest heavily in this technology. They innovated by creating their own content, which set them apart from their competitors.

However, they did not stop there. Netflix continued to adapt by using data analytics to inform its product strategy. They looked at what their customers were watching and what they wanted and used this information to create new content and features. They also pivoted their business model by eliminating their DVD-by-mail rental service and focusing solely on streaming.

This approach paid off for Netflix, now one of the most prominent players in the entertainment industry. By innovating and adapting, they could stay relevant and provide their customers with what they wanted.

Innovation and adaptation are essential elements of keeping your startup relevant. You can ensure success by fostering a culture of creativity, staying up-to-date with industry trends, listening to your customers, being willing to pivot, and responding quickly to changes.

Remember that innovation does not necessarily mean creating something wholly new but improving what you already have. Adapting means being flexible and willing to change your business model, products, services, or processes. By employing innovation and adaptation, you can stay ahead of the curve and create a loyal customer base that appreciates your value.

Chapter Nineteen
Overcoming Obstacles: Common Mistakes and Challenges

Starting a new business is always challenging. It is a challenging endeavor with many obstacles and hurdles, some of which may seem insurmountable. However, you can overcome any obstacle and build a successful startup with the right mindset, determination, and a good strategy. This chapter will explore some common mistakes and challenges that startups face and how you can overcome them.

Common Mistakes

Starting a new business is risky and requires significant time, effort, and resources. Unfortunately, many entrepreneurs need proper planning to approach their startup, which can lead to success. Here are some of the most common mistakes that startups make.

1. Lack of Clarity

One of the most significant mistakes startups makes is the need for more clarity about their goals and objectives. In addition, many entrepreneurs need a clearer understanding of their target audience, products, and services. With a clear focus, developing a compelling value proposition and differentiating your business from the competition can be easier.

Solution: Before starting your business, take the time to define your goals and objectives. Conduct market research to identify your target audience and understand their needs and pain points. Finally, develop a clear value proposition that differentiates your business from the competition and provides a compelling reason for customers to choose your products or services.

2. Poor Financial Management

Another common mistake that startups need to improve is poor financial management. Proper financial planning and management make staying afloat in a competitive market easier. Many entrepreneurs need to pay more attention to unnecessary expenses or allocate sufficient resources to essential aspects of their business.

Solution: Create a detailed financial plan that includes projected revenue and expenses for the first few years of your business. Identify areas where you can save money and prioritize investment in critical aspects of your business, such as marketing, product development, and customer support.

3. Lack of Focus on Customer Needs

A common mistake entrepreneurs make is focusing too much on their products or services and needing more on customer needs. It is essential to understand the needs and preferences of your target audience to develop products and services that meet their needs and provide a positive customer experience.

Solution: Conduct extensive market research to identify customer needs and preferences. Use this information to develop products and services that meet their needs and provide a positive customer experience. Implement customer feedback mechanisms to stay in touch with your customers and continually improve your products and services.

4. Poor Marketing Strategy

Another common mistake that startups need to improve is a better marketing strategy. Proper marketing makes it easier to attract customers and build brand awareness. Many entrepreneurs must pay more attention to word-of-mouth referrals or effective marketing strategies.

Solution: Develop a comprehensive marketing strategy that includes traditional and digital marketing channels. Identify the most effective channels for your target audience and focus your efforts on those channels.

Continuously track and measure the effectiveness of your marketing efforts and make adjustments as necessary.

Challenges

Starting a business takes work, and there will be many challenges. Here are some of the most common challenges startups face and how to overcome them.

1. Funding

One of the most significant challenges that startups face is funding. Starting a business requires considerable investment in product development, marketing, and other essential aspects of the company. As a result, many entrepreneurs need help to secure funding, which can hinder their ability to grow and succeed.

Solution: Explore various funding options, including venture capital, angel investors, and crowdfunding. Develop a detailed business plan outlining your objectives, projected revenue, and expenses. This plan will help you attract potential investors and demonstrate the viability of your business.

2. Competition

Another common challenge that startups face is competition. In today's highly competitive market, differentiating your business and standing out can be challenging. Many entrepreneurs need help to compete with well-established companies with more extensive resources and a larger customer base.

Solution: Develop a unique value proposition differentiating your business from the competition. Emphasize your special features and benefits and highlight what sets you apart from the competition. Focus on providing exceptional customer service and building strong relationships with your customers.

3. Hiring and Retaining Talent

Hiring and retaining top talent is another significant challenge that startups face. Unfortunately, many startups need help attracting and retaining talented employees who are essential to the success of their business. Without a skilled and motivated workforce, it can be challenging to grow and succeed.

Solution: Develop a strong company culture that values and supports employees. Offer competitive compensation packages and opportunities for career growth and development. Focus on creating a positive work environment that promotes collaboration, innovation, and creativity.

4. Scaling

Scaling your business can be a significant challenge for startups. Managing and maintaining the same quality and customer service can be challenging as your business grows. In addition, scaling requires significant investment in resources and infrastructure, which can be difficult for startups with limited resources.

Solution: Develop a comprehensive growth strategy to scale your business. Identify potential growth opportunities and build the necessary infrastructure and resources. Then, continuously monitor and adjust your growth strategy as your business expands.

Starting a new business is a challenging endeavor with many obstacles, including funding, competition, and scaling. However, you can overcome any obstacle and build a successful startup with the right mindset, determination, and strategy. By avoiding common mistakes and addressing common challenges, you can increase your chances of success and take your business to new heights.

Chapter Twenty
Success Stories: Real-Life Examples of From Idea to Reality

Starting a business from scratch requires an idea, a plan, and much hard work. Unfortunately, while many entrepreneurs pour their hearts and souls into their startups, only a few succeed. However, the ones who do succeed can serve as an inspiration for others who are embarking on the same journey.

This chapter will explore some real-life success stories of startups that have turned their ideas into reality. These stories demonstrate that anything is possible with the right mindset, skills, and team.

1. Airbnb – A Simple Bed-and-Breakfast Idea That Changed the World

Airbnb was founded in 2007 by three friends – Brian Chesky, Joe Gebbia, and Nathan Blecharczyk – who were struggling to pay their rent in San Francisco. They came up with the idea of renting out air mattresses in their apartment so that people could have a place to sleep during a local design conference.

The idea was a hit, and the three friends realized they were onto something big. So they launched Airbnb, a website that allowed people to rent out their spare rooms or entire homes to travelers. Today, Airbnb is worth over $100 billion and has helped millions worldwide find affordable and unique accommodations.

2. Warby Parker – Disrupting the Eyewear Industry with Affordable Glasses

Warby Parker was founded in 2010 by four friends – Neil Blumenthal, Dave Gilboa, Andrew Hunt, and Jeff Raider – who were frustrated by the high eyewear prices. So they decided to create a company that offered stylish and affordable glasses that could be purchased online.

Warby Parker disrupted the eyewear industry by cutting out the middleman and offering direct-to-consumer sales. The company is worth over $3 billion and has become a household name in the eyewear business.

3. Spotify – Changing the Way We Listen to Music

Spotify was founded in 2006 by two Swedish entrepreneurs – Daniel Ek and Martin Lorentzon – who wanted to create a better way to listen to music online. So they launched Spotify, a streaming service that gave users access to millions of songs for free or a small monthly fee.

Spotify disrupted the music industry by allowing people to listen to music on demand without buying individual songs or albums. Today, the company has over 345 million active users and is worth over $50 billion.

4. Zoom – Making Video Conferencing a Household Name

Zoom was founded in 2011 by Eric Yuan, a former executive at Cisco who wanted to create a video conferencing service that was easy to use and affordable. Zoom was launched in 2013 and quickly became a popular tool for businesses and individuals who wanted to connect remotely.

Zoom's popularity skyrocketed during the Covid-19 pandemic, as millions worldwide had to work and study from home. Today, the company is worth over $100 billion and has become a household name in video conferencing.

5. Patagonia – Building a Sustainable Business

Patagonia was founded in 1973 by Yvon Chouinard, a rock climber and environmentalist who wanted to create a sustainable business that made high-quality outdoor gear. Patagonia has always been committed to reducing its environmental impact and promoting ethical labor practices.

Today, Patagonia is worth over $1 billion and has become a leader in the sustainable fashion industry. The company has also launched numerous initiatives to promote environmental activism and protect public lands.

6. Tesla – Disrupting the Auto Industry with Electric Cars

Tesla was founded in 2003 by Elon Musk, who wanted to create a car company that would help reduce our dependence on fossil fuels. Tesla launched its first electric car, the Roadster, in 2008 and has since become a leader in the electric car industry.

Tesla has disrupted the auto industry by creating high-performance electric cars that are both stylish and eco-friendly. Today, the company is worth over $800 billion and has become a symbol of innovation and sustainability.

These success stories demonstrate that anything is possible with the right idea, the right team, and much hard work. While entrepreneurship is not easy, it can be incredibly rewarding for those willing to take risks. These startups have not only changed their respective industries but have also changed the world in their way.

Epilogue

As the final pages of "From Idea to Reality: The Complete Startup Handbook" are turned, the journey of creating a successful startup doesn't end. Instead, it is a continuous journey fueled by the ideas that inspired the startup in the first place.

The ideas in this book have been gathered from some of the most innovative entrepreneurs who have blazed a trail in their respective industries. They have faced challenges, overcome failures, and always have sight of their vision.

The book is not intended to provide a quick-fix solution but a comprehensive guide to the startup world, from finding the right business model to funding, marketing, hiring, and product development. It is a roadmap, a valuable tool for anyone who dreams of being their boss and creating a thriving business.

The most important takeaway from this book is to embrace the startup journey for what it is: a roller coaster of ups and downs. It is not for the faint of heart but for those willing to push forward and persevere.

The end of this book marks the beginning of a new chapter of the startup journey. The entrepreneurs who have read this book are now equipped with the knowledge and tools to take their ideas to the next level.

They should remember that every successful entrepreneur once stood in their shoes, full of uncertainty but driven to make something happen. So, as they take their first steps, they should take comfort in knowing they are not alone in their journey.

They should also embrace and learn from any startup journey's inevitable failures and setbacks. Success is not always linear or predictable, but it is attainable for courageous and persevering people.

In the end, the accurate measure of success is not the money earned or the fame achieved but the satisfaction of creating something that makes a difference in the lives of others. Whether it is a product, a service, or an idea, the world needs entrepreneurs willing to take the leap and turn their ideas into reality.

About The Author

Claudia Lowry is an entrepreneur, business consultant, and virtual administrator.

Born in South Africa, she had several start-up companies and franchises that taught her the skills and expertise she needed to grow and sell her companies successfully.

Today she has helped thousands of business owners streamline their business systems and discover ways to work efficiently and effectively to live the life they love… spending their valuable time doing the things that matter most to them.

If you want to explore ideas that could work for you and your business, go to https://tidycal.com/claudialowry to book a no-cost consultation.

www.ingramcontent.com/pod-product-compliance
Lightning Source LLC
Chambersburg PA
CBHW070919220526
45467CB00004B/1476